D1575253

To:

From:

A Simple Guide to

Happiness

Written and compiled by

Barbara Paulding

Illustrations by **Lauren Wan**

PP PETER PAUPER PRESS, INC.
White Plains, New York

To my mom, who lived a good life

Designed by Rebecca Lown
Illustrations copyright © Lauren Wan 2009

Copyright © 2009
Peter Pauper Press, Inc.
202 Mamaroneck Avenue
White Plains, New York 10601
All rights reserved
ISBN 978-1-59359-836-5
Printed in China
21 20 19 18

Visit us at www.peterpauper.com

A Simple Guide to

Happiness

Contents

Introduction

This simple guide to happiness is your SparkNotes to renewal. This is not rocket science. "Simple" and "happiness" are words that belong together. Complexity may be good for keeping the mind sharp, but happiness is hardly ever that fancy. In these pages you'll find guidance and inspiration to walk the path of sacred silliness. You'll learn how the practice that cultivates happiness is an endeavor that blossoms and spreads exponentially—like those liquid crystal forests—but lasts a whole lot longer. And you'll learn that happiness is not a tame beast that can be pursued and captured, but rather, as E. L. Konigsburg writes, an "excitement that has found a settling down place. But there is always a little corner that keeps flapping around."

Much as positive psychology has turned its focus to optimum living and happiness, we can allow ourselves the prospect of joy, making choices that facilitate a happy life. Modern neuroscience has the tools to study which parts of the brain are activated while in a state of well-being and peace. Positive psychologists have determined that, while about half of our state of content or discontent depends upon a genetically determined "set point" and about ten percent derives from our life's circumstances, the rest we hold in our hot little hands—created out of our thoughts, actions, and attitude. It's up to us to make choices that invite the bluebird of happiness to nest in our hair. This little book is about those choices, chapter by chapter.

I've been talking about happiness not as a trait but as a skill, like tennis. If you want to be a good tennis player, you can't just pick up a racket—you have to practice.

—Richard Davidson

Savor the Moment

A giant step toward living a happy life has to do with being willing to play the "get out of jail free" card. Underlying the whole untidy mess of our lives are beliefs about worthiness and capability. Can we allow ourselves happiness? And are we capable of sustaining it? There's no redeeming value to feeling guilty or unworthy of joy. We best serve our world by shining our light. Hold that thought.

The other gremlin of malcontent is called perfectionism. Many of us strive to be beyond rebuke, make perfect choices, look very smart. The message to this gremlin, and its close cousin, the "if only," is: pipe down. Perfectionism is overrated, and "if only" is a myth. When we trust ourselves to make reasonable choices and move on, we claim the freedom to breathe.

Savor the moment. Be mindful when you eat, walk, drive, converse. Meditate. On brain maps created by neuroscientists, meditation increases brain activity in the region linked to positive emotions. Happy people live in the zone of the here and now.

Consider the lilies of the field. . . .
Read in the backyard with
the sun on your face.
Learn to be happy.
And think of life as a
terminal illness, because,
if you do, you will live
it with joy and passion,
as it ought to be lived.

ANNA QUINDLEN

If you observe a really happy man
you will find him building a boat,
writing a symphony, educating his son. . . .
He will not be searching for happiness
as if it were a collar button that
has rolled under the radiator.
He will have become aware
that he is happy in the course
of living life twenty-four crowded
hours of the day.

W. BERAN WOLFE

The universe is full
of magical things
patiently waiting
for our wits to
grow sharper.

EDEN PHILLPOTTS

Precisely the least,
the softest, lightest,
a lizard's rustling,
a breath, a flash,
a moment—a little
makes the way of
the best happiness.

Friedrich Nietzsche,
Thus Spake Zarathustra

Our life is shaped
by our mind; we
become what we think.
Joy follows a pure
thought like a shadow
that never leaves.

BUDDHA

There are lots of things to
see, unwrapped gifts and
free surprises. The world
is fairly studded and strewn
with pennies cast broadside
from a generous hand.

ANNIE DILLARD

I ask you, what is the use of having your "cake" if you can't eat it? What exactly are you supposed to do with it?... Cake is meant to be eaten and enjoyed.

T. HARV EKER

Happy Body, Happy Head, Happy Heart

I think by now we can all agree on the body-mind principle, and the fact that our mind and matter influence each other. After all, quantum physics has shown that matter broken down to its most infinitesimal components is energy, and thought is energy, so it rather goes without saying that our thoughts affect our bodies, and our bodies affect our minds. Just as we can work to tame the gremlins of the mind, we can enhance our physical well-being. This begins with the choice.

Body care is an exercise in sensibility. Get enough sleep. Nurture yourself with healthful foods. Exercise in a way you enjoy enough to do regularly—start off the day with your own private dance party, for instance. Stretch like a cat whenever you get up. And don't forget to breathe.

Happiness
pulses with
every beat
of my heart.

EMILY LOGAN DECENS

Dance is the
hidden language
of the soul
of the body.

MARTHA GRAHAM

A sound mind in
a sound body is a
short but full description
of a happy state in
this world.

JOHN LOCKE

Good for the body is
the work of the body,
good for the soul the
work of the soul,
and good for either
the work of the other.

HENRY DAVID THOREAU

Advantages to being
fully present in the body
are those moments when
we can get down to
the experience of
pure Being—of Bliss.

E. KATHERINE KERR

Happiness consists of...
comfortably going
through everyday life,
that is, having had a good
night's sleep and not being
hurt by new shoes.

THEODOR FONTANE

Joy is a return to the deep harmony of body, mind, and spirit that was yours at birth and that can be yours again.

DEEPAK CHOPRA

Judging from accounts of…
exceptional performance by
athletes and artists, we harbor
a greater life than we know.
There we go beyond those
limited and limiting patterns…
that have been
keeping us in drydock.
In this state we know
great torrents of delight.

JEAN HOUSTON

Practice Kindness

Kindness is compassion in action, a principle that benefits the giver as much as it does the recipient. Religious and humanitarian groups have long known what science is recently documenting: that volunteering and doing for others not only serves a need, it enhances well-being. In other words, it feels good. Helping out reinforces our belief that we're capable of helping out, that we have something worthwhile to give. It engenders a sense of camaraderie and common purpose.

But kindness does not require a committee. It's about showing up. The casual compliment to a colleague who seems down, a visit to a nursing home relative, homemade cookies for a new neighbor, listening deeply and without judgment to a troubled friend—these are valuable gifts that require little fanfare. If our kind deeds utilize our special talents or strong suits, and if they vary from week to week, they will create an even greater sense of happiness.

*In about the
same degree
as you are
helpful you
will be happy.*

CARL REILLAND

The best way to
cheer yourself
up is to try to
cheer somebody
else up.

MARK TWAIN

Every time
you smile at someone,
it is an action
of love, a gift
to that person,
a beautiful thing.

MOTHER TERESA

Three things in
human life are
important. The first is
to be kind. The second
is to be kind. And the
third is to be kind.

HENRY JAMES

I slept and dreamt
that life was joy.
I awoke and saw that
life was service.
I acted and behold,
service was joy.

Rabindranath Tagore

The place to be happy
is here. The time to
be happy is now.
The way to be happy
is to make others so.

ROBERT G. INGERSOLL

If you want others to be

happy, practice compassion.

If you want to be happy,

practice compassion.

THE DALAI LAMA

Work Deeply

If you can do what you love as your life's work, do it! You are one of the lucky ones who has a calling that can support you. But if Plan A eludes you, reframe your work to give it more meaning and variety. Since life is not a dress rehearsal, invest in each moment by being fully engaged in what you're doing. Trot out your best self to enjoy the satisfaction of a job well done. If you can't do what you love, love what you do. Let your heart sing.

Use your strengths in a variety of ways in your job. Notice if your values and life goals are in harmony with your work. The working life is rife with opportunities to practice kindness, patience, humor, gratitude, and acceptance, all of which cultivate the pearl of happiness.

The biggest mistake
people make in life is
not trying to make a
living doing what
they most enjoy.

MALCOLM S. FORBES

A path without a heart
is never enjoyable.
On the other hand,
a path with heart is easy—
it does not make a
warrior work at liking it;
it makes for a joyful journey;
as long as a man follows it,
he is one with it.

CARLOS CASTANEDA,
The Teachings of Don Juan

43

No matter what your
occupation, let what you
are doing be organic.
Let it be in your bones.
In this way you will open
the door by which the
affluence of heaven and
earth shall stream into you.

RALPH WALDO EMERSON

Success is not the key
to happiness. Happiness
is the key to success.
If you love what you
are doing, you will
be successful.

ALBERT SCHWEITZER

45

What I know is,
is that if you do work
that you love,
and the work fulfills you,
the rest will come.

OPRAH WINFREY

Make a new commitment
to think of your work not as
a place to make a living,
but as an opportunity
to make a life. . . .
The whole Universe is on
your side, guiding your hands
and directing your footsteps
in the way you go.

ERIC BUTTERWORTH

Work is love made visible.
And if you cannot work
with love but only distaste,
it is better that you should leave
your work and sit at the gate of
the temple and take alms of
those who work with joy.

KAHLIL GIBRAN

Find Your Tribe

In a world that has become increasingly compartmentalized into individual or family units, our innate need for community sometimes goes unmet. We are primates looking for our band, social creatures adrift in a crowd of strangers, edging ever closer to the shadows of alienation. To light a candle against the darkness, engage in activities you care about deeply. You'll become part of a social network of like minds, people who share the same passion as you—your tribe.

A key to social satisfaction isn't quantity; it's quality. The depth of friendship matters, creating a space in which souls commune. As Mark Twain wrote, "To get the full value of a joy you must have somebody to divide it with."

The most I can do
for my friend is simply
to be his friend.
I have no wealth to
bestow on him.
If he knows that
I am happy in loving
him, he will want no
other reward.

HENRY DAVID THOREAU

Thousands of candles
can be lighted from
a single candle,
and the life of the candle
will not be shortened.
Happiness never decreases
by being shared.

BUDDHA

53

Look carefully around you
and recognize the luminosity
of souls. Sit beside those
who draw you to that.

R U M I

Let us be grateful
to people who make us
happy; they are the
charming gardeners who
make our souls blossom.

MARCEL PROUST

I cannot even imagine
where I would be today
were it not for that
handful of friends who
have given me a heart
full of joy. Let's face it,
friends make life a lot
more fun.

CHARLES R. SWINDOLL

All real living

is meeting.

MARTIN BUBER

We humans are social beings.... There is hardly a moment of our lives when we do not benefit from others' activities. For this reason it is hardly surprising that most of our happiness arises in the context of our relationships with others.

THE DALAI LAMA

There is nothing we like to see so much as the gleam of pleasure in a person's eye when he feels that we have sympathized with him, understood him. At these moments something fine and spiritual passes between two friends.

DON MARQUIS

The Gratitude Attitude

Feeling grateful for what you have shifts attention from what you may lack, places you in the present moment, and works against the tendency to take even wonderful things for granted. This is the simple key to the joy of gratitude. Being thankful involves a certain humility, too, taking us out of the ego, which so often moves us away from happiness.

Make gratitude a habit, however it suits your style. Keep a journal in which you honor the gifts in your life. Take time at the end of each day to practice a gratitude meditation, in which you visualize each object of appreciation while allowing your heart to meet it. Count your blessings. Write a letter of thanks to someone who has made a positive difference in your life.

Happiness cannot be
traveled to, owned,
worn, or consumed.
Happiness is the
spiritual experience
of living every minute
with love, grace,
and gratitude.

DENIS WAITLEY

*Be content with
what you have;
rejoice in the
way things are.
When you realize there
is nothing lacking,
the whole world
belongs to you.*

LAO TZU

If the only prayer you
say in your life is
"thank you,"
that would suffice.

MEISTER ECKHART

Happiness
is itself
a kind of
gratitude.

JOSEPH WOOD KRUTCH

*Gratefulness is the key
to a happy life
that we hold in our hands,
because if we are not grateful,
then no matter how much
we have we will not be happy.*

BROTHER DAVID STEINDL-RAST

Both abundance and lack
exist simultaneously in our lives,
as parallel realities.
It is always our conscious choice
which secret garden we will tend.…
When we choose not to focus on
what is missing from our lives
but are grateful for the
abundance that's present…
the wasteland of illusion falls away
and we experience Heaven on earth.

SARAH BAN BREATHNACH

In our daily lives,
we must see that it
is not happiness
that makes us grateful,
but the gratefulness
that makes us happy.

ALBERT CLARKE

Live Large

Make life more meaningful by engaging in a realm larger than yourself—spiritual life, religion, art, politics, science, teaching, nature, running marathons, or whatever holds value for you. Life is not a tame critter, and we can't control the outcome. But as we lose ourselves in the culture and ideas of a field that really matters to us, our sometimes puny and circular minds spin out of a rut. There is something more than all the busy goings-on in daily life, and it is something great and worthwhile.

The joy of being a cell in the greater being of spirit, art, nature, or whatever it is, paradoxically is both a comfort and a challenge. We feel akin to it, but at the same time we're never sure what it will require of us, or if we can deliver. It stretches us, and it brings us home. There's a magic and a familiarity to this place, and we have had the ruby slippers to take us here all along.

Many people have a wrong idea of what constitutes true happiness. It is not attained through self-gratification but through fidelity to a worthy purpose.

HELEN KELLER

The pleasures of a good conversation,
the strength of gratitude,
the benefits of kindness or wisdom
or spirituality or humility,
the search for meaning and the
antidote to "fidgeting until we die"
are the birthrights of us all.

MARTIN E. P. SELIGMAN

Life is infinite
creative play;
enjoyment and
participation
in this creative
play is the artist's
profound joy.

ALEX GRAY

Climb the mountains
and get their good tidings.
Nature's peace will flow into you
as sunshine flows into trees.
The winds will blow their own
freshness into you . . . while cares
will drop off like autumn leaves.

JOHN MUIR

This is the true joy in life,
the being used for a purpose
recognized by yourself
as a mighty one;
the being a force of nature
instead of a feverish selfish
clod of ailments and
grievances complaining that
the world will not devote itself
to making you happy.

GEORGE BERNARD SHAW

The best remedy for those who are
... unhappy is to go outside,
somewhere where they can
be quiet, alone with the heavens,
nature and God. Because only
then does one feel that all is as it
should be and that God wishes to
see people happy, amidst the
simple beauty of nature.

ANNE FRANK

Sacred space and sacred
time and something joyous
to do is all we need.
Almost anything then
becomes a continuous
and increasing joy…
I think a good way to
conceive of sacred space
is as a playground.
If what you're doing seems
like play, you are in it.

JOSEPH CAMPBELL

O to have my life
henceforth a poem
of new joys!
To dance, clap hands,
exult, shout, skip, leap,
roll on, float on,
To be a sailor
of the world,
bound for all ports,...
A swift and
swelling ship,
full of rich words—
full of joys.

WALT WHITMAN